# Train up a Child: Bible stories for childre

Copyright © 2018 by Maroon Warrior Publishing LLC

Written by Zaab Benjamin

Art and Illustration by Aaron Hunter and Jonathan Pryor

Contributions from: The Lions of Israel

All rights reserved. Printed in the United States of America. No part of this book may be used or reproduced, stored in a retrieval system, or transmitted by any means, electronic, mechanical, photocopying, recording, or otherwise, without written permission from the publisher. Although every precaution has been taken in preparation of this book, the publisher and author assume no responsibility for errors or omissions.

Contact Information for The Lions of Israel:

Web address: www.TheLionsofIsrael.com

E-mail: ThelionsofIsrael@gmail.com

Call: **877-535-4667**

Publisher Information:

Maroon Warrior Publishing LLC

547 North Ave, Suite #178

New Rochelle, NY 10801

Web address: www.maroonwarrior.com

E-mail: contactinfo@maroonwarrior.com

# The Lions of Israel

# <u>Acknowledgements</u>

First and foremost, we give all honor and praises to The Most High, Yahawah, in the name of His son, Christ (Yahawahshi). This is a work created by The Lions of Israel. Many thanks to the elders: Danyaahla Benjamin, Chazaaq Gabar, Rawchaa Karath, Nagayahana, and Deacon Iyshayar. Shalam to the captains; Tahan, Mahgan, Yawanathan, and Banyawasap. Salute to the brothers Abraham, Hapshipyah, Elijah, Ahmath, James and Yawasap. Shalawam to the elders Chaarab, and Thomas.

To the brothers of A.O.C, I Am Israel, Apostles of New Jerusalem, U.K.O.I, H.O.W, F.O.P.E, Sons of Yahawah, House of Israel, House of David, Light of Zion, Shield of Wisdom, and to ALL the Churches and camps teaching the truth; shalawam. Lastly, to all the people who labor with us in the hopes of waking our people up and sealing the elect of The Most High, may He bless you in the name of His son.

Shalawam.

Zaab Benjamin

# Foreword

Shalam family. This chief reason why this book is created is because of the lack of realistic and historical children's books geared towards the future of our nation. We are living in the age where outright lies and deceitful propaganda are being taught to our little ones. It is our duty, and job, as parents who know the truth, to teach our offspring the history about who we are and our rightful place on this Earth. We are the children of The Most High. The promises and the giving of the law, and the covenants were made with us (**Romans 9:4**).

The title of this work is '**Train Up a Child**' taken from the book of **Proverbs**, chapter 22, verse 6: *train up a child in the way he should go: and when he is old, he will not depart from it.* This is our sole focus; to reach the youth who will one day be the men and women of our nation. If we teach them while they are babes, they will grow up to carry on the righteous doctrines and traditions of our forefathers as it is written in the holy scriptures.

We wrote this book with you, and your sons and daughters in mind. If not us, then who? No one, outside of our nation, will take the effort to do this. We are all that we have until we are delivered out of this captivity by the hand of The Lord. Until then, we cannot have our enemies corrupting the minds of our posterity. (**Apocrypha, Ecclesiasticus 30:3**, *he that* teacheth his son grieveth the enemy...).

On behalf of Lions of Israel, we thank you for your support. May this book serve as a spark that ignites the mind of the child who reads this. To have them inquire about The Most High, and all the works He has done for our people, Israel (Yahsharahla), and to see yourselves as a great and mighty nation equal to none. The scriptures tell us that when we are in order, and keeping the commandments of our Power, there is no nation that can dare to stand against us **(Apocrypha, Judith 5:17-18)**. The Earth was created for us and we should not forget it.

Thank you (thawadah) for your donation and your support. May The Most High, Yahawah, in the name of His son, Yahawahshi, bless you. Shalam.

*The Lions of Israel.*

# <u>Note</u>

\* *The God of Abraham, Isaac, and Jacob has a name. That name is **YAHAWAH**. It is pronounced as it sounds phonetically. When writing in ancient Hebrew, the vowels are omitted, and the spelling is **YHWH**.*

*English is not our original language. It is a hybrid of different languages and creates problems when translating words and phrases from an original language. Some words simply cannot be translated into English, and if they do, they lose their meaning.*

\*\* *The word **Christ**, which is Greek, means anointed. The Son of God has a name: in Hebrew, when translated, is **Yahawahshi** (some pronounce it as **Y'shua**). We use the Paleo, or ancient Hebrew, to give us the closest and most accurate spelling and pronunciation. We do **not** use Jehovah or Jesus; reason being is the letter '**J**' does not exist in the Hebrew language.*

*Please do your own research for yourselves as the scriptures tells us to: '**Prove all things; hold fast that which is good**' (1 Thessalonians 5:21). Hebrew is the language of our forefathers. The patriarchs, the prophets, and the Messiah all spoke Hebrew.*

\*\*\**We also quote from the **Apocrypha**; books that were originally part of the canon of the King James 1611 Bible.*

# *The Creation of the World*

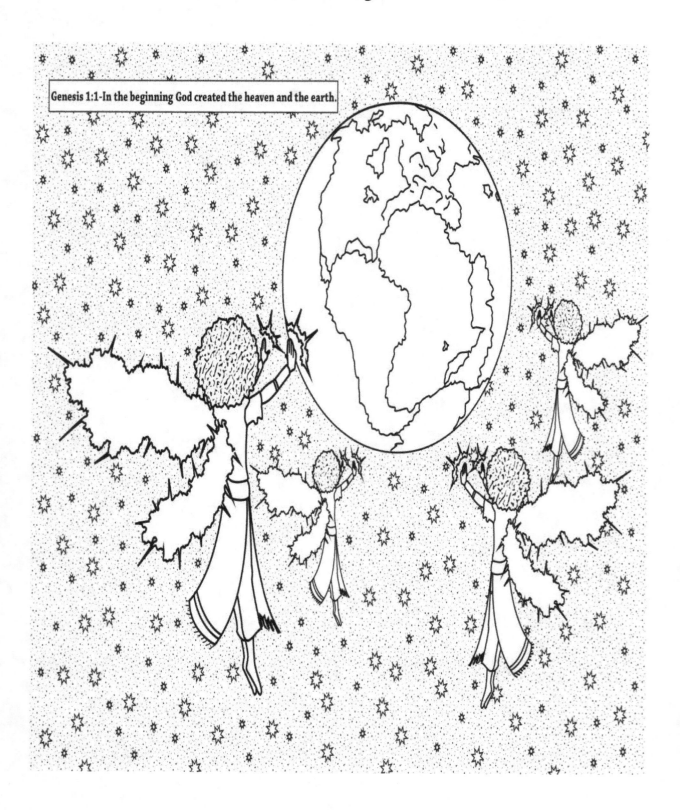

Genesis 1:1-In the beginning God created the heaven and the earth.

I n the beginning, The Most High (YAHAWAH) created the heaven and the earth *(Genesis 1:1)*. There was darkness, and nothing was formed. There were no trees, no blue skies, no animals, no birds, no insects, or any water. God, the Father, gave the blueprint to Yahawahshi, (Christ) the son, and the angels, to create the heaven and the earth.

*And God said, let there be light: and there was light.* He divided the light from the darkness. The light he called Day and the darkness He called Night. That was done on the first day. Before there was any life as we know it on the planet, The Most High, through Christ and the angels, created everything in existence *(St. John 1:1, Hebrews 1:2)*. In the original Hebrew, *Genesis 1:1*, the word for God is **Ahlahayam** which means power(s) plural. Yahawahshi (Christ), and the angels were there.

Today our children are taught scientific 'theory' that life was created from an explosion and evolution. Those are crafty lies created by the father of lies, the devil himself, to try and displace The Most High and corrupt our children's mind. If we teach them the truth, then the enemy will not win *(Apocrypha, Sirach 30:3)*.

When we observe the beauty of the world we can see there is a supreme being. Everything has its purpose and season and are thankful for Him *(Psalms 19:1-2)*.

# *Adam and Eve*

GENESIS 3:1-5

A nd the Lord God formed man of the dust of the ground, and breathed into his nostrils the breath of life; and man became a living soul *(Genesis 2:7)*. He was made in His image, meaning he was given the laws of The Most High, making Adam the first righteous man. Eve was created as well to be his wife *(Genesis 1:27, 2:18)*. Together, the Lord commanded them to be fruitful and multiply.

The problems start, as it usually does throughout the scriptures and in our personal life, when we disobey the Heavenly Father and choose to do our own thing. The serpent tricked Eve into believing lies, and she broke the commandment by eating of the tree of the knowledge of good and evil **(Genesis 2:17)**. She then gave to her husband Adam, who also broke the commandment by eating of the tree as well.

Adam and Eve tried to hide from the Lord when they heard Him walking in the garden. But, just like a true father, He knew what they did before even asking. The Lord punished them by removing them out of the garden because of their actions.

It is a good thing to do right so that The Most High will bless you with eternal life, and you will inherit His righteous kingdom on Earth.

# CAIN AND ABEL

Genesis 4:8-And Cain talked with Abel his brother: and it came to pass, when they were in the field, that Cain rose up against Abel his brother, and slew him.

Cain and Abel were brothers who lived a long time ago. Adam and Eve were their mother and father. Abel was the keeper of the sheep, but Cain was a tiller of the ground **(Genesis 4:2)**. They both offered sacrifices to The Most High. Cain brought an offering form the fruit of the ground, and Abel the firstlings of his flock 'and of the fat thereof'. The Most High chose Abel's offering over Cain's and as a result Cain was mad.

**(Genesis 4:6-7)** *'And the Lord said unto Cain, Why art thou wroth? And why is thy countenance fallen? If thou doest well, shalt thou be not accepted? And if thou doest not well, sin lieth at the door'.*

Even though The Most High told Cain the truth he still disobeyed. One day, he killed his own brother. *(Genesis 4:8 and 1 John 3:11-15).* Cain was the first murderer in the sight of The Heavenly Father; not only that, but he was also a liar. *(Genesis 4:9) And the Lord said unto Cain, where is Abel thy brother? And he said, I know not: Am I my brother's keeper?*

The Lord cursed Cain for his wicked deeds and made him a fugitive and a vagabond in the earth.

# NOAH'S ARK

GENESIS 7:6 And Noah [was] six hundred years old when the flood of waters was upon the earth. 7 And Noah went in, and his sons, and his wife, and his sons' wives with him, into the ark, because of the waters of the flood. 8 Of clean beasts, and of beasts that [are] not clean, and of fowls, and of every thing that creepeth upon the earth, 9 There went in two and two unto Noah into the ark, the male and the female, as God had commanded Noah.

Noah was a man who The Lord found grace in, especially when people were doing evil at that time. All the people in the earth were going off and following their own vein imaginations.

Noah was born hundreds of years after Adam and Eve. The earth was a different place from when the Lord first created man and placed him in the garden of Eden. Because sin entered the world, men grew wicked and the Lord was very upset.

*(**Genesis 6:6-7**) "And it repented the Lord that he had made man on the earth, and it grieved him at his heart. And the Lord said, I will destroy man whom I have created from the face of the earth; both man, and beast, and the creeping thing, and the fowls of the air; for it repenteth me that I have made them."*

It is important to note that the sins (transgressions against the law – **1st John 3:4**) that were being committed back then are still being done today. Our lord Yahawahshi (whom the world ignorantly calls Jesus Christ) told us that this would happen. Read **Luke 17:26-27**.

# Abraham's Sacrifice

GENESIS 22:9-12 And they came to the place which God had told him of; and Abraham built an altar there, and laid the wood in order, and bound Isaac his son, and laid him on the altar upon the wood. And Abraham stretched forth his hand, and took the knife to slay his son. And the angel of the Lord called unto him out of heaven, and said, Abraham, Abraham: and he said, Here am I. And he said, Lay not thine hand upon the lad, neither do thou any thing unto him: for now I know that thou fearest God, seeing thou hast not withheld thy son, thine only son from me.

Abraham was a man highly favored of The Most High. He had only one son by the name of Isaac whom he loved dearly. The Lord told Abraham to sacrifice Isaac to show his loyalty and love to Him *(Gen 22:1-18)*. Abraham obeyed The Most High without question, showing his faith as an obedient servant.

It is hard in this day and time to comprehend the faith Abraham had for The Most High by doing His will without question. Sometimes our parents ask us to do things that we cannot understand right away, but we should know that they mean the best for us. We should strive to be like Abraham.

As we read on in the story, The Most High saw that Abraham obeyed him and provided a ram to sacrifice instead of Isaac. He also blessed Abraham by multiplying his seeds (children) as the stars of heaven, and as the sands on the sea shore *(Gen 22:17)*. This shows us that there is great reward in doing the will of The Father.

Children should obey their parents, as it is written in the book of the law **(Exodus 20:12)**. There is great reward in keeping The Most High's commandments. Trust in The Lord and good things will be bestowed on you.

# *Sodom and Gomorrah*

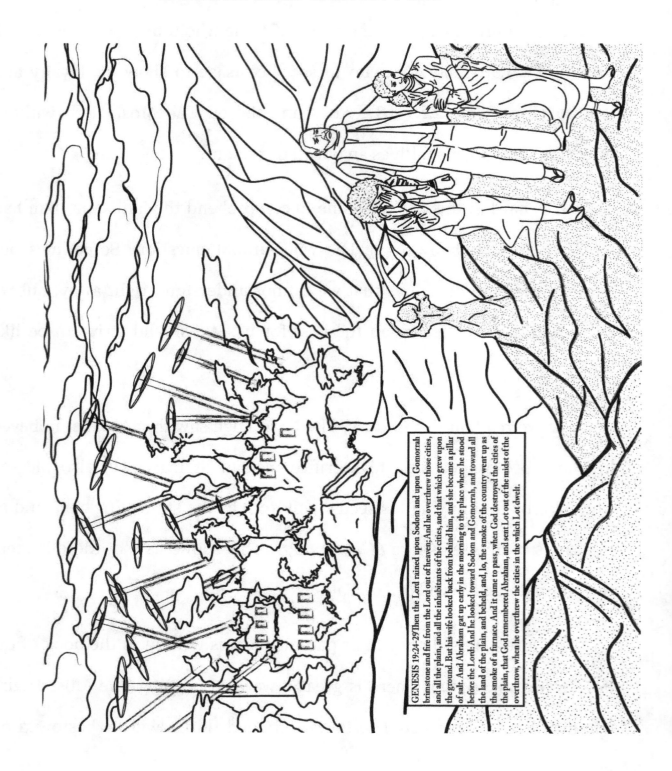

GENESIS 19:24-29 Then the Lord rained upon Sodom and upon Gomorrah brimstone and fire from the Lord out of heaven; And he overthrew those cities, and all the plain, and all the inhabitants of the cities, and that which grew upon the ground. But his wife looked back from behind him, and she became a pillar of salt. And Abraham gat up early in the morning to the place where he stood before the Lord: And he looked toward Sodom and Gomorrah, and toward all the land of the plain, and beheld, and, lo, the smoke of the country went up as the smoke of a furnace. And it came to pass, when God destroyed the cities of the plain, that God remembered Abraham, and sent Lot out of the midst of the overthrow, when he overthrew the cities in the which Lot dwelt.

The bible speaks of a wicked place called Sodom and Gomorrah that existed a long time ago. This was a place of physical, and spiritual wickedness. One day, two angels visited the town and they were met by a rigthtious man named Lot. The evil people of the town also came out to prey upon the angels who looked like men. **Genesis** the **19**th chapter tells the entire story.

The angels told Lot to gather his family and loved ones because The Lord has sent them to destroy the city off the face of the earth. In the morning Lot, his wife, and two daughters were brought out of the city to safety right before the judgement began. The angels told Lot to flee to the mountains, and DO NOT LOOK BACK! That was a very specific instruction as we will soon see.

Then the Lord rained upon Sodom and Gomorrah fire and brimstone out of heaven *(Gen 19:24)*. **But Lot's wife looked back and was changed into a pillar of salt**. Again, we see that obeying The Lord gives life and disobeying brings death. The smoke from the destruction of that city rose up high in the sky as smoke from a furnace; so shall the modern-day Sodom and Gomorrah be destroyed as well.

# *The Passover*

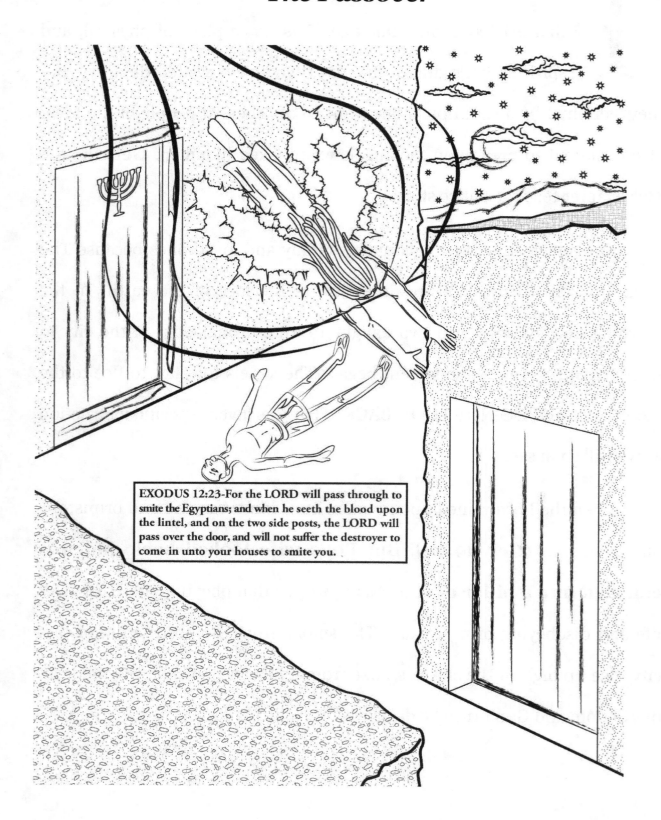

EXODUS 12:23-For the LORD will pass through to smite the Egyptians; and when he seeth the blood upon the lintel, and on the two side posts, the LORD will pass over the door, and will not suffer the destroyer to come in unto your houses to smite you.

Exodus the 12th chapter tells the story of the Passover. This is when the Lord killed all the first born of the Egyptians but passed over the houses of the Israelites who had the blood of a sacrificed lamb painted on their door post. This is a wonderful, great work the Lord did to free us from captivity and we commemorate this event every year.

During this time a man by the name of Moses was chosen by the Lord to lead our people out from the hard bondage of the Egyptians. Pharaoh, the king of the Egyptians, refused to let us go to serve our Lord. He put us under a system of slavery without the shackles, like how we are today. We cried out to The Lord and He heard our prayers and delivered us.

The Lord sent different plagues on the Egyptians; but Pharaoh would not let us go until the final plague killed all the firstborns in the land of Egypt *(Exodus chapters 8-12)*. Finally, we were free to serve our God.

Every year we are commanded to keep a feast to remind us of how we were delivered out of bondage *(Ex 12:14)*. On the 14th day of the first month (Abib), at sundown, we kill the sacrificial lamb and have a feast. We also do **not** eat bread made with yeast to symbolize how we left Egypt in haste; not having time to let the bread rise. Read the wonderful history in **Exodus** chapter **12**.

# The Commandments

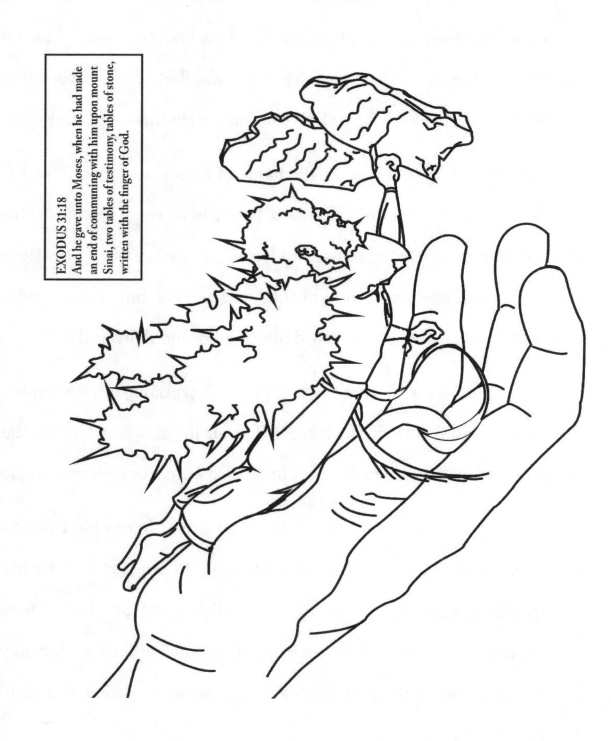

EXODUS 31:18
And he gave unto Moses, when he had made an end of communing with him upon mount Sinai, two tables of testimony, tables of stone, written with the finger of God.

After the children of Israel came out of Egypt, we were judged by Moses in the name of The Most High. We received a righteous written covenant between us and The Lord of Hosts; that we will be His people, and He will be our Power.

On the sacred mountain of Sinai, Moses received the commandments to give to **us**, the Israelites. ***Exodus, the 19th and 20th*** chapter, tells how the Lord came down in a cloud and spoke directly to Moses; and gave him the law. Not only did the Lord give the law, but also the judgement and penalties for those who broke it. The Lord gave Moses two tablets of stone, upon which the commandments were written with His finger ***(Exodus 31:18)***.

Our people are a hard-headed people. We forsook the Lord and worshipped a golden calf while Moses was away ***(Exodus 32:1-6)***. When he returned, he was so upset that he broke the tablets. This is an example of how our people can be rebellious. Imagine how the Lord saved us from the slavery of Egypt, only to have us disobey Him once we became free?

Moses had to go back up the mountain and plead with the Lord to forgive us, and to keep the promise He made to our forefathers; Abraham, Isaac, and Jacob.

# *David and Goliath*

1Samuel 17:45-50-David said to the Philistine, "You come against me with sword and spear and javelin, but I come against you in the name of the LORD Almighty, the God of the armies of Israel, whom you have defied. This day the LORD will hand you over to me, and I'll strike you down and cut off your head. Today I will give the carcasses of the Philistine army to the birds of the air and the beasts of the earth, and the whole world will know that there is a God in Israel. All those gathered here will know that it is not by sword or spear that the LORD saves; for the battle is the LORD's, and he will give all of you into our hands." As the Philistine moved closer to attack him, David ran quickly toward the battle line to meet him. Reaching into his bag and taking out a stone, he slung it and struck the Philistine on the forehead. The stone sank into his forehead, and he fell facedown on the ground. So David triumphed over the Philistine with a sling and a stone; without a sword in his hand he struck down the Philistine and killed him.

The book of *1ˢᵗ Samuel* tells the story of David, one of the mightiest warrior Kings that ever lived. He was courageous from the time of his youth and faithful to The Most High. He showed his courage, skill, and faith by killing Goliath; an enemy of our people, with a sling and a stone.

At that time the nation of Israel was at war with the Philistines. They had a giant by the name of Goliath that fought for them, and everyone feared him. David was the youngest son of Jesse and keeper of his father's flock. One day, David brought food to his brothers that were in the battle and saw the giant speaking badly about our people. David showed his courage by stepping up to fight the giant for the Lord, and our people.

Being only a youth with no military experience, he did not use a sword, he used the weapon that he knew. He used a sling and a stone to fight *(1ˢᵗ Samuel 17:40)*. As he drew near to Goliath, David told him that this day the Lord has delivered him into his hands. He put a stone in his sling and struck Goliath with it. The giant fell on the ground and David cut his head off. He showed faith by not being afraid and trusting in the Lord.

In life we should put our trust in the Lord to guide us to victory in whatever we set out to do. Read the story in *1ˢᵗ Samuel*, the *17ᵗʰ* chapter.

# Daniel in the Lion's Den

Daniel 6:16-24

Daniel was a servant of the Lord who lived in the time when the Persians ruled over our people. The king of the Persians name was Darius and he admired Daniel a lot. He made Daniel a ruler in his kingdom; but some Persians were jealous of him and tried to find a way to discredit Daniel.

The wicked Persian princes and rulers came up with an idea to trick the king into harming Daniel. They knew Daniel was a righteous man who prayed to The Most High and kept the laws and commandments. They told the king that he should make a decree that no one should pray to God for thirty days *(Daniel 6:7).* If they did, whomever was caught would be thrown into the lion's den. Daniel heard about this decree and still went and prayed to the heavenly Father, as he normally did three times a day *(Daniel 6:10)*.

When the jealous rulers told the king, Daniel was thrown into the lion's den. The angel of the Lord saved Daniel from being hurt by the lions. When the king saw he was untouched the next day, he rejoiced and praised The Most High who delivered Daniel. Because they tried to trick the king, he threw the jealous princes into the den and the lions ate them, and their families. We must do what is right by The Lord no matter what the consequences are. He will deliver us just as he delivered Daniel.

# *Jonah in the belly of the whale*

JONAH 1:17 Now the LORD had prepared a
great fish to swallow up Jonah. And Jonah was
in the belly of the fish three days and three nights.

J onah had a visit from the word of the Lord telling him to go to the land of Nineveh. But he disobeyed and tried to run away, thinking he could hide from the creator of heaven and earth. He got on a ship to sail to away, but the Lord stirred up the winds and seas so much that the people on the ship were afraid.

Everyone prayed except Jonah because he knew that he was the reason for the storm. He told them to throw him overboard into the sea so that they could live because they would not be safe. The Lord prepared a large fish for Jonah and it swallowed him up alive. He was in the belly of the fish for three days and three nights *(Jonah 1:17)*.

Jonah prayed while he was in the belly of the fish and the Lord heard him and delivered him. Then Jonah went on his journey and did what the Lord asked of him. He went to Nineveh and prophesied to the people that the city would be destroyed in forty days if they do not repent from their wicked acts. The people repented, and the Lord did **not** destroy them.

When the Lord gives you a task you should obey and do it. Also, if your parents tell you to do something, (seeing that they care for you and love you like the Lord) you should take heed and do it too.

# *Birth of Yahawahshi (Christ)*

MATTHEW 1:18-25 Now the birth of Jesus Christ was on this wise: When as his mother Mary was espoused to Joseph, before they came together, she was found with child of the Holy Ghost. Then Joseph her husband, being a just [man], and not willing to make her a publick example, was minded to put her away privily. But while he thought on these things, behold, the angel of the Lord appeared unto him in a dream, saying, Joseph, thou son of David, fear not to take unto thee Mary thy wife: for that which is conceived in her is of the Holy Ghost. And she shall bring forth a son, and thou shalt call his name JESUS: for he shall save his people from their sins. Now all this was done, that it might be fulfilled which was spoken of the Lord by the prophet, saying, Behold, a virgin shall be with child, and shall bring forth a son, and they shall call his name Emmanuel, which being interpreted is, God with us. Then Joseph being raised from sleep did as the angel of the Lord had bidden him, and took unto him his wife: And knew her not till she had brought forth her firstborn son: and he called his name JESUS.

The birth of our Lord Yahawashi, who we ignorantly called Christ, was special because it meant that salvation came for Israel. He was sent to save **his** people **(Matthew 1:21)** from **their** sins. He had a father, Joseph, and a mother Mary. They both made him just like your father and mother made you – the natural way. He came through the bloodline of Judah, the same as king David *(Matthew 1:1-17)*.

More importantly, his birth signifies that we are free from the sacrificial laws of Moses (which were a shadow of things to come *Hebrews 10:1-10*), and from transgressions that required the blood of bullocks and other animals to atone us back to The Most High. We are still required to keep the commandments as even Christ told us *(John 14:15)*.

Yahawahshi (Christ) was born like the rest of us but he is special and different from us. Angels came and prophesied to Joseph and Mary letting them know their son had a great destiny to fulfill. Mary carried the baby the same time as any woman carries a child and gave birth the same way. Wise men came from afar to pay respect and brought precious gifts. Each Israelite child birth is special, just like yours, but baby Yahawahshi's was the most unique ever in the creation of time.

# *Miracles of Yahawahshi (Christ)*

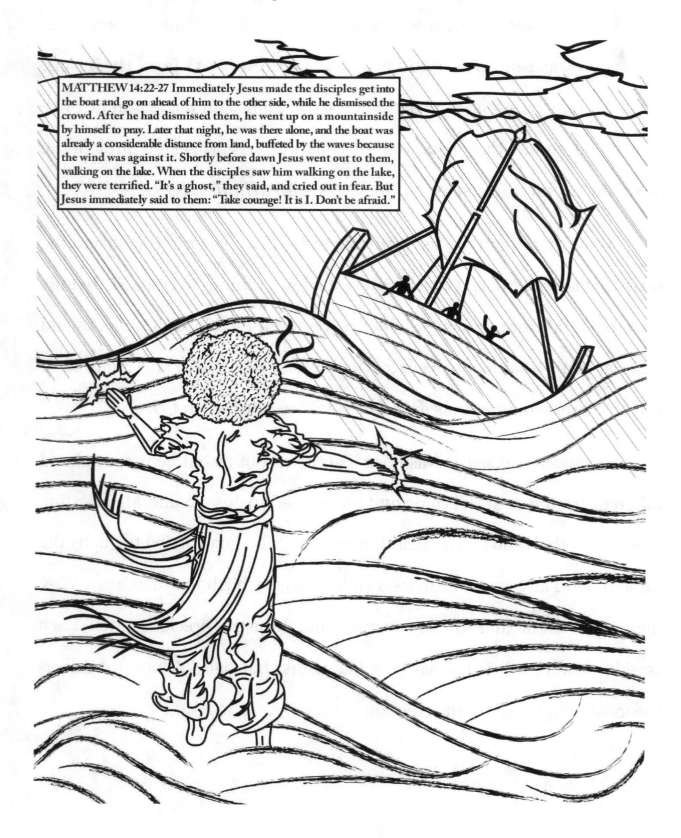

MATTHEW 14:22-27 Immediately Jesus made the disciples get into the boat and go on ahead of him to the other side, while he dismissed the crowd. After he had dismissed them, he went up on a mountainside by himself to pray. Later that night, he was there alone, and the boat was already a considerable distance from land, buffeted by the waves because the wind was against it. Shortly before dawn Jesus went out to them, walking on the lake. When the disciples saw him walking on the lake, they were terrified. "It's a ghost," they said, and cried out in fear. But Jesus immediately said to them: "Take courage! It is I. Don't be afraid."

When Yahawahshi walked the earth, he performed many miracles and healed his people, the Israelites. His job was to bring us back to The Most High by giving his life as a sacrifice, but first he had to make them believe that he was truly the messiah prophesied to save us.

He changed water to wine *(John 2:1-8)* at a wedding, fed a multitude of people with just five loaves of bread and two fish *(Matt 14:19),* and many other great things for Israel. One of the miracles he performed was to walk on water. His disciples were on a ship offshore and he walked on water out to meet them. When they saw Yahawahshi they were afraid, and Peter asked to come unto him; to see if it was really him. Peter started to walk on water at first, but lost faith seeing the rough weather and began to sink. Yahawahshi helped him up and told him to have faith *(Matthew 14:23-33).*

In everything we do we must have faith. If Peter had kept his faith he would have continued to walk on water. Yahawahshi told us in *Matthew 17:20*; if we have faith, even as small as a mustard seed we can do great things. Faith is required to serve The Father; and without it we can do nothing. The book of *Hebrews, chapter 11 verse 1* sums it all up: *now faith is the substance of things hoped for, the evidence of things not seen.*

# *Death of Yahawahshi (Christ)*

LUKE 24:19-21 And he said unto them, What things? And they said unto him, Concerning Jesus of Nazareth, which was a prophet mighty in deed and word before God and all the people: And how the chief priests and our rulers delivered him to be condemned to death, and have crucified him. But we trusted that it had been he which should have redeemed Israel: and beside all this, to day is the third day since these things were done.

As the bible taught us, Yahawahshi died for our sins, the nation of Israel (Yahsharahla). There are many scriptures that prove this; *Acts 5:31*, *Romans 9:1-5*, *Matthew 15:24*, *Luke 22:28-30*, *Joel 2:32*, *Isaiah 45:17*, are among the few.

He fulfilled his mission which was to be a sacrifice for our sins. He was crucified on a cross, and a Roman soldier pierced his side with a spear. Even when he died miracles were still being worked: the temple veil was torn in two, and people came out of their graves *(Matthew 27:50-53)*. Yahawashi made the ultimate sacrifice for his people, so we can have remission of sins. Even those opposed to him recognized it and knew it *(John 11:50)*.

Can you think of a personal sacrifice you made that helped others? This is the example that he set forth for us to follow; to think of others before ourselves. Yahawahshi taught us that we should love The Lord with all thy heart, and all thy soul, and with all thy mind; and we should love our neighbors as we love ourselves *(Matthew 22:36-40)*.

Yahawahshi also taught us a lesson about forgiveness. He forgave the Israelites who plotted on his life *(Luke 23:39)*. As an example, we should forgive those of our people who try to do harm to us.

# *Resurrection of Yahawahshi (Christ)*

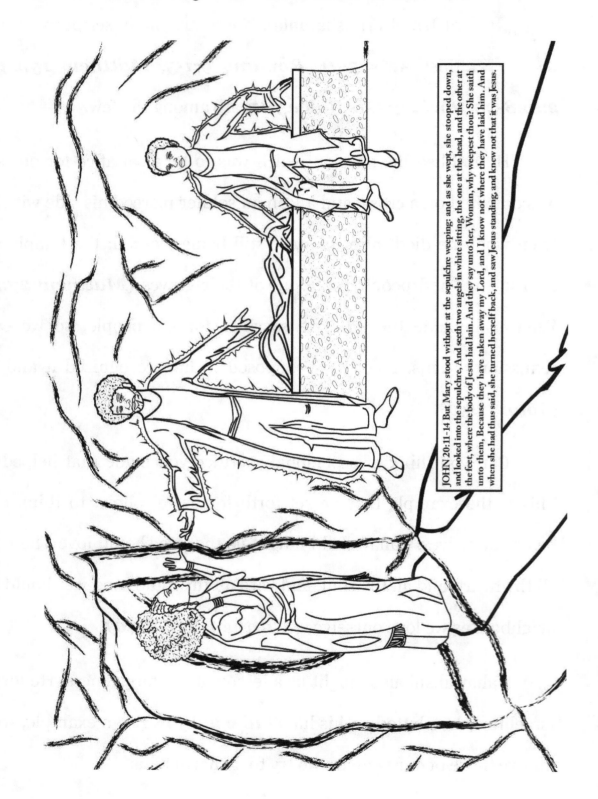

JOHN 20:11-14 But Mary stood without at the sepulchre weeping; and as she wept, she stooped down, and looked into the sepulchre, And seeth two angels in white sitting, the one at the head, and the other at the feet, where the body of Jesus had lain. And they say unto her, Woman, why weepest thou? She saith unto them, Because they have taken away my Lord, and I know not where they have laid him. And when she had thus said, she turned herself back, and saw Jesus standing, and knew not that it was Jesus.

Yahawahshi completed his mission, and fulfilled prophecy, when he died for Israel's sins. Now he had to be delivered from the grave to show that death could not have power over him *(Romans 6:9)* and to show himself alive. He told the people what would happen before time. Just like Jonah was in the belly of the whale for three days and three nights, so shall the Son of man be in the heart of the earth *(Matthew 12:40)*.

Mary Magdalene was the first to see that Yahawahshi was risen from the dead. She then ran and told his disciples, and they ran to see the empty grave. All that remained were the clothes he wore. They left Mary as she wept for our Lord. She looked and saw two angels sitting in the place where Yahawahshi laid. Christ appeared to her, but she didn't recognize him until he told her it was him *(John 20:1-18)*.

Yahawahshi revealed himself to his disciples at different times and performed great miracles after he rose from the dead. He showed them the holes in his hands and the hole in his side. He also revealed scriptures from the law of Moses, the prophets, and the Psalms concerning him *(Luke 24:40-45)*. He was seen of many and Israel knew that the promise of The Father was fulfilled, and remission of sins preached in his name.

# *Ascension of Yahawahshi*

Acts 1:9-11 And when he had spoken these things, while they beheld, he was taken up; and a cloud received him out of their sight. And while they looked stedfastly toward heaven as he went up, behold, two men stood by them in white apparel; Which also said, Ye men of Galilee, why stand ye gazing up into heaven? this same Jesus, which is taken up from you into heaven, shall so come in like manner as ye have seen him go into heaven.

After he finished his ministry and works, Yahawahshi left the people he came to save. He was transported up to heaven in a cloud *(Acts 1:9)*, which we ignorantly call a U.F.O. These are the same chariots that the angels use to travel back and forth. We also know that Elijah was taken up in a 'whirlwind' *(2 Kings 2:11)*, and Yahawahshi will return with the same chariots *(Isaiah 66:15)*.

In modern times, like the days we are living in, we seem to think that the things we experience now, our ancestors did not. In some cases; such as the internet we do, but for the most part there is nothing new under the sun.

The bible speaks of Yahawahshi ascending to heaven by way of a cloud to sit at the right hand of The Most High *(Mark 16:19)*. This is the same way that the elect shall be saved from the time of destruction. Our lord died for the nation of Israel's sins. He was resurrected and went up to be with our Father *(Psalms 110:1)*. He shall return the same way *(Acts 1:10-11)*. We should all strive to be like him and keep his commandments as an example to our brothers and sisters *(John 14:15)*.

When Christ returns he will not be a sacrifice, but a warrior coming to deliver his people. The lord will vanquish our enemies.

# *Rapture*

REVELATIONS 11:12-And they heard a great voice from heaven saying unto them, Come up hither. And they ascended up to heaven in a cloud; and their enemies beheld them.

When the bible speaks about a rapture we should understand that those of us who live to see Yahawahshi return will be caught up, or "beamed" up to the clouds, aka chariots, to meet him *(1 Thessalonians 4:17)*. We will leave this world and all the evil things in it behind. The Lord will come back to deliver his people from all corners of the earth *(Matthew 24:30-31)*. Yahawahshi, the messiah, will send his angels to gather his people together and save them from the judgement of the nations.

He told us to be ready because he can return at any time. No one knows exactly when, but we should be prepared *(Luke 12:40)*. We do this by showing love to one another, and by keeping his commandments that will bring us closer to The Heavenly Father. The commandments are a guide, or tools, when followed will help you to stay on the right path. Ultimately Christ is our savior and go between to get to The Most High *(1 Timothy 2:5)*.

By having faith, and by good works, The Most High will send us Christ. He will deliver us *(Revelation 3:10)*, the Israelites, from the bad times that are coming. It will be a glorious sight to see the elect of our people being delivered to meet him. We should all strive to be counted in that number. The ones who died for the truth shall be risen first.

42

# <u>Closing</u>

Israel (Yahsharahla), we thank you for getting this book and supporting The Lions of Israel to push the Word of The Most High. Our job as teachers, parents, and family members, is to first and foremost raise up our children the right way according to the scriptures *(Proverbs 22:6)*. Lord willing, when they get older they will not depart from righteous instructions. It is up to us to instill divine values in our children.

The scriptures speak of the righteous being vexed with the conversation of the wicked *(2nd Peter 2:7-8)*: as a parent so should we. Our history is not being taught in the school system. Instead, all manner of idolatry, perversion, and carnal deviancy is being pushed on our little ones. The purpose of this book is to illustrate the truth about our biblical history, so we can see ourselves as the royal and righteous people that we once were and will be again. So-called blacks, Latinos and Native Americans (whose fathers are negro or native Indians) are the real Israelites that the bible speaks of. It is paramount and vital that we read about our forefathers to instill self-worth, and positive self-esteem. The writings of the apostle Paul describe it best in the book of *Romans chapter 15, verse 4: For whatsoever things were written aforetime were written for our learning, that we through patience and comfort of the scriptures might have hope.*

Ahbanawa **YAHAWAH** ba ha sham **Yahawahshi** barak athum (may The Most High bless you in the name of Christ).

Shalam

Printed in the USA
CPSIA information can be obtained
at www.ICGtesting.com
LVHW071046211123
764451LV00025B/516